Zebras & Ostriches:

5 Simple Rules to Engage and Retain Your Best People

Philip Kim

three boys press

Zebras & Ostriches:
5 Simple Rules to Engage and Retain Your Best People

Published by:
Three Boys Press, a subsidiary of Ideapath Consulting, LLC,
Canal Fulton, Ohio.

First Edition

Printed in the United States of America

For book ordering or permission requests, write or email the publisher, at the address below:

Ideapath Consulting, LLC
9751 Diamond Ridge Circle
Canal Fulton, OH 44614
www.ideapathconsulting.com

Praise for *Zebras & Ostriches: 5 Simple Rules to Engage and Retain Your Best People...*

"Good things do come in small packages! Within this short book are some incredible gems to help you create a more engaged and productive workforce."

■ **Shep Hyken**
New York Times Bestselling Author of *The Amazement Revolution*

"In your hands you hold a blueprint for a new way of thinking and a better way of acting on your way to becoming the leader you were meant to be. How you inspire people to grow will make you indispensable in your career!"

■ **Mark LeBlanc**
Author of Never Be the Same and Growing Your Business!

"In a more and more interconnected world, technical expertise is no longer the determining factor as to why someone will work with and/or for you. Talent is just a Google or LinkedIn search away. People have always done biz with and/or for people they know, like, and trust. Phil's book explains a simple approach to creating a culture of passion, enthusiasm, and value. Sincere relationships always have been and always will be the determining factor of top performing people and organizations. This book should be required reading for everyone in the workforce."

■ **Kevin Knebl**
Recognized by LinkedIn as the *Most Recommended Business Speaker in the World*. Co-Author of *The Social Media Sales Revolution*

"We are better together and together we can accomplish amazing things. Read this simple, power book and build a high performing team!"

■ **Jon Gordon**
Wall Street Journal Bestselling Author of *The Energy Bus*

"To make powerful ideas into something that is simple and easy to apply, while making it entertaining is a definition of sophistication and art. This little book is an example of that. Read on and enjoy."

■ **Kordell Norton, CSP**
Speaker and Author of *Business Charisma: How Great Organizations Engage and Win Customers Again and Again*

"*Zebras & Ostriches* is classic Phil Kim. On-point, practical, funny, human...and all business. If you're looking for a quick read that filters out the fluff and gets right to the heart of how to keep your people engaged this is it. It's full of gems and perfect for any time-strapped business owner or manager."

■ **Chuck Violand**
President and CEO, Violand Management Associates

"Who knew businesses were filled with Zebras and Ostriches? This quick read provides powerful insights into employee engagement and actionable items you can implement immediately. Any leader will benefit from reading Phil's book."

■ **Steven Burger, CPA, MBA**
Chief Financial Officer, Employers Health

Dedication

To Amanda.

And to our three precious boys: Be good.

To all leaders who seek to inspire their teams.
Stay the course.

Table of Contents:

Preface:
Zebras and Ostriches

Did you know that Zebras and Ostriches both live in the southern African savanna? They actually live and graze together too. For some reason when I think of these two animals, I never put them together. Yet, they are very closely and intimately intertwined.

Zebras have notoriously bad vision, but have an acute sense of smell. Ostriches have a bird's eye view, but can't smell danger. These two animals forage and travel together in pods in order to warn each other of incoming predators.

This is a natural symbiotic relationship that keeps both animals safe from harm. It's a harmonious bond because their strengths and weaknesses are complementary. They could compete for the same resources, and see each other as adversaries, but that would defeat the purpose of traveling together. Think about this, these are two completely different species of animal, and yet they live together and cooperate towards a common goal: survival.

As a leader, your employees are not that much different. Your organizations are filled with Zebras and Ostriches. It's your job to ensure they function together as a team.

All of your employees have unique skills and potential areas of improvement. The key is to leverage those strengths and to provide a framework for them to be most successful.

Everywhere I go I hear the same refrain: companies are constantly worried about finding and retaining the right people. Some people don't fit, some people are great, but they leave too soon. Some people are skilled but can't handle the pressure. Managers are spending an inordinate amount of time, money, and resources trying to find and replace their best employees.

Zebras & Ostriches: 5 Simple Rules to Engage and Retain Your Best People is a book that provides a simple, practical, and real-world approach to increase the level of employee engagement, productivity, and commitment within your organization.

This short book is the summary of my research during the past five years since I've left my corporate position as the head of Information Security for a multi-billion dollar financial services institution. As a speaker and consultant I've had the privilege to present my workshops to numerous companies ranging from Fortune 500 companies to family-owned enterprises to non-profit and service-based organizations.

The truth remains: every leader is continually seeking to engage and retain their best people.

Regardless of industry, size, or existing company culture, these simple but profound insights will help you increase your employee engagement.

Let me be clear, it will take some work to make it fit your particular organization and culture. Don't lose heart if things take longer than you expect. When you are trying to establish a new way of doing something, it will be met with resistance. As a leader you have to be willing to take some risks and let some of your people go. It's not that they're bad people, they're just not the right fit for your team.

The feedback from this book and my presentations has been very encouraging. People want to work with other people who are excited to be on the same page. My favorite responses are:

"I can't wait to go back to my office and implement these techniques!"

"I didn't realize how much of an impact I can have on the engagement of other people outside of my department!"

It's been said that people join companies, but leave managers.

I agree with this. Maintaining productive relationships is a critical component to increasing productivity and engagement. And sometimes you have to let people go so they can find a team that's a better fit. It's addition by subtraction. One of the worst things you can do for an employee is keep them around, because you'll feel badly for letting them go. Think of it more like you're finally setting them free.

Set Them Free

From 1991 to 1995 Bill Belichik was a nobody. Before he became the 3x AP NFL Coach of the Year and a 4x Super Bowl Champion as a head coach, he was the coach of the lowly Cleveland Browns where he compiled a record of 36 wins and 44 losses. In five full seasons with the Browns, Belichik had one playoff appearance, a loss to the Pittsburgh Steelers. If he would have stayed with the Browns, there is no doubt in my mind – he would be out of the league by now.

But he didn't stay. He was set free and eventually able to get a job with the New England Patriots in 2000. His firing ultimately landed Belichik in the perfect environment for him to learn and grow, and become a shoe-in for first-ballot Hall of Fame honors. The rest is Spygate-Deflategate-Super Bowl history.

If your employees aren't adding value to your organization, it means they are not the right fit for you. By all means set them free, so they can find their place. The sooner they find a career that engages them, the better for both parties. This book isn't really about getting rid of people, it's about keeping your best employees and letting them shine.

I want your organization to be filled with the best Zebras and Ostriches you can find and for you to keep them engaged so they'll never want to leave.

Chapter 1:

Any Monkey Can Do What You Do

Have you ever had a job you really hated? I mean truly could not stand?

I was hired by a publicly traded financial service provider to start their internal IT Audit function. I was particularly excited for this position because it was a promotion from my old job, and it was an opportunity to work for a very well-respected company within the community. In fact, this company has repeatedly been recognized as one of the "Top 100 Places to Work" in Pennsylvania.

I probably should have realized something was wrong when I first I joined the company. My boss was never around! For two weeks I had no one to report to. After a few days, I scheduled some meetings in order to get a lay of the land. I wanted to meet my co-workers and look at what projects needed to get started. Finally, after 14 days, my boss returned to work and asked me to come into her office.

She told me the following gems of insight:

"Philip, you're different than the others, and I don't like that."

"You were not my first choice for hire."

"I don't know how you used to do it, but around here there's a certain culture and you don't fit."

And then there was this pithy quip:

"I've seen your previous work. Any monkey can do what you do."

Whoa.

So, I guess I'm not getting that Christmas bonus?

Did she just call me a monkey?

I had no idea where this was coming from, but from that day forward, everything was different. The glow of working for a "Top 100 Company" was completely gone. I can still remember the uneasiness and dread I would feel every evening before work the next day. I was stressed, couldn't sleep, and gained a lot of weight. I can remember some of my close friends saying, "Phil, you've changed. Why don't you smile anymore?"

I didn't know what to do. I felt trapped.

On the outside, everything looked fine. I had finally been hired by one of the exemplar companies in the industry and the job was in the town my wife and I wanted to live in. It was a good, respectable job with solid pay and benefits. I should have had no complaints.

No Confidence

It wasn't the company. It was my boss. I had absolutely no confidence that my supervisor had my best interests in mind. In fact a few weeks after my "you're no better than a monkey" pep talk, my boss brought me in for another special "coaching" session. Maybe she felt badly about the last meeting and wanted to mend some fences?

She explained that she was still "concerned" for me because I had "high social requirements" and constantly needed to "talk with others."

Not good.

Note the personal attack on who I was as a person.

Think about this for a moment.

I was hired to start up a completely new function within this organization. How else was I supposed to understand what the existing process was without talking to people? This was a primary function of my job, to interview key stakeholders to get the most accurate information.

The reason I was completely disengaged from my job had **nothing to do with the work itself**. Believe it or not, I actually like auditing. In fact even eight years after I left that department, I still admire and fundamentally believe in the IT Audit profession.

My active disengagement was solely based on the lack of trust and awkward relationship with my direct supervisor. I became more worried about not making her mad and trying <u>not to get fired</u> than I was about trying to add value to the organization. I was in self-preservation mode.

What a waste of my time and the company's resources!

I was so disappointed, because this was supposed to be my ideal job.

Your Best People Will Leave

Take a moment and recall all of your past jobs. Are there any where you felt like a fish out of water?

If you take a deeper look into why you couldn't connect at your job it was probably one of three reasons:

1. You didn't like your boss,
2. You didn't like your co-workers, or
3. Your skills and talents weren't being optimally utilized.

For over 10 years I struggled with one or all of these reasons at every job I've had – regardless of job title, employer, or salary range. Don't get me wrong, I still worked hard, did my best, and was somehow able to advance my career throughout those years.

You don't have to "love" something to do it well. But there was always something consistently nagging inside me to find something different. When that voice got too loud, the easiest thing for me was to simply put out my resume and look for another job.

Leaving a job is so easy now. Even in a challenging economy, if your best employees are motivated enough, they will find a way to leave.

That's why employee engagement is so important to me. Regardless of the latest training workshops, materials, or modern tech gizmos – if your best employees are not engaged – they will not perform their best, and eventually find somewhere else. And your company will have squandered its resources on training and development that could have been used elsewhere.

Are you losing your best people?

Would you even know?

Seven out of 10 people are either dissatisfied with their work or are actively trying to leave your company. [1]

The bad news is leaders that don't take an active and intentional step towards engaging their employees, the turnover and attrition rates will continue to rise – and organizations will be losing their best people to the competition.

The good news is this doesn't have to be you.

As a leader, you can have a direct impact on the level of engagement of your employees.

The even better news is you can start implementing these 5 Rules of Engagement today.

The best news is, these rules can be implemented for free.

Chapter 1 Notes:

1. Gallup (2013).
   http://www.gallup.com/businessjournal/162953/tackle-employees-stagnating-engagement.aspx.

Chapter 2

What is Employee Engagement?

To begin we should have a clear understanding of what I mean by employee engagement.

An "engaged employee" is one who is fully absorbed by and enthusiastic about their work and as a result takes positive action to further the organization's reputation and interests.

An organization with 'high' employee engagement might therefore be expected to outperform those with 'low' employee engagement, all else being equal. [1]

Discretionary Effort

Similar to discretionary money or time, employees who are engaged will be willing to put forth extra effort and attention towards moving the organization forward.

Are your employees willing to give discretionary effort?

"Discretionary effort is the level of effort people could give if they wanted to, above and beyond the minimum required. Many organizations manage performance in such a way that motivates employees to do only enough to get by and avoid getting in trouble (negative reinforcement). Typically, these organizations manage by exception, providing consequences for worker's performance only when it falls below the standard or minimum required. This approach gets immediate results, but *just enough* behavior to stop the threats and the potential for other negative consequences in the near future. It suppresses discretionary effort because there's nothing in it for people to do more than the minimum required." [2]

Does it Matter?

The latest Gallup Organization's employee engagement research report that only 30% of employees are actively engaged at their jobs. Which leaves 70% that are not engaged, or actively disengaged at their work. More recent news has even less encouraging numbers reporting the percentage of actively engaged employees to be as low as 18%.

Have you ever worked with someone who is actively disengaged? They are not simply satisfied with sabotaging their own careers, they want to take others down with them. In fact actively disengaged employees cost the US over $500 billion in lost productivity every year.

What do most leaders do?

If you're being honest, you ignore, marginalize, or move them to another department. Thus further perpetuating the vicious cycle of passing off a bad employee to another part of the company.

According to Eric Koester of MyHighTechStart-Up, "estimates range from 1.5x to 3x of salary for the 'fully-baked' cost of an employee - the cost including things like benefits, taxes, equipment, training, rent, etc." Hiring a new employee isn't a decision that should be taken lightly, as it doesn't fall lightly on the company budget. [3]

By the time you factor in the cost of recruiting, training, onboarding, and lost productivity, you can see why it's easier and cheaper just to let bad employees stick around.

The Lake

One of my favorite co-workers of all time was a crusty old man by the name of Frank. Frank was a great guy and a very hard worker. In a lot of ways he was the model employee. He commuted over an hour to work, but was never late. He did everything he was asked to do and worked hard at meeting all of his deadlines. If you were to ask Frank what he loved about work he would say "that's easy, the lake."

What in the world is the lake?

The lake is Frank's oasis away from work. Actually it's his primary source of enjoyment in life. You can always tell when Frank has a story about the lake because his eyes start to twinkle. He has a wife (married over 30 years), two grown kids and a number of grandchildren – but he'll be the first to tell you his one true love is the lake.

He's got a double-wide trailer on a "little slice of heaven" as he calls it. I've seen pictures. It's a trailer on the side of very steep hill. If this is heaven, I'm not interested. He has a very-used and beat-up pontoon boat on his dock on Raystown Lake in Huntingdon County, PA. This location has all the conveniences of his primary residence and he's able to live there eight months out of the year. Every weekend the lake isn't frozen – you know where you can find Frank.

He works so he can go to the lake. He goes to bed early so he can go to the lake. He's willing to suffer a multi-hour drive from Johnstown, PA to Indiana, PA five days a week so he can experience the peace and solitude of the lake on Saturday and Sunday.

This is discretionary effort. Everything he does in life revolves around the lake.

If he thinks about spending extra money or going out to lunch with his co-workers, in the back of his mind he's doing a quick cost-benefit analysis. He's not cheap. He spends money. It's just all of his money go towards being at the lake. He'll think *could this lunch money be better used to repair something on the boat or buy another gadget for the lake house? Do I need more beer for the lake house?* Everything depends on the lake.

On top of this, whenever his co-workers like me or other colleagues saw anything related to the lake, we would enthusiastically tell him about it!

Hey Frank, there is this really cool bug spray that lasts all day and you don't even smell it!

Hey Frank, I found this singing bass wall mount at a garage sale and I had to get it for you.

Imagine if your employees were as enthusiastically engaged about your organization as Frank was about his lake?

Isn't that the kind of people you want working for your organization? A few devoted employees that are dedicated to the organization can increase the overall level of productivity and morale of other team members.

Employee engagement is a workplace approach designed to ensure that employees are committed to their organization's goals and values, motivated to contribute to organizational success, and are able at the same time to enhance their own sense of well-being. [3]

Employee Satisfaction is a Myth

I was recently speaking with a healthcare executive about the topic of employee engagement. As we were discussing some of the challenges in her organization, something struck me. Here I was talking about increasing engagement in order to increase employee retention, but she was dealing with completely uninspired employees. Free loaders, social loafers, moochers, the Costanzas – whatever you want to call them: these are the drones that are simply there to cash a check.

Are they satisfied? Absolutely. In fact, they are so satisfied, they don't do anything! They've become used to cruising at their jobs. I felt her pain as I know a few colleagues in my profession that are very "satisfied" with their jobs and probably should have retired a long time ago.

We've heard that satisfied employees are happy employees. Especially within the health care fields, we've all heard that satisfied health care providers lead to satisfied patients.

Taken out of context, this is a total myth.

She lamented that satisfaction surveys showed these employees were extremely satisfied but showed no initiative to getting anything done.

Employee satisfaction is good, but without engagement it's useless. Don't confuse satisfaction with engagement.

So if you're in this situation, what can you do to increase engagement?

It's time to raise the bar.

If these employees were good at some point in their careers, I would argue they've simply lost their way. They need to be given a chance to find themselves again. Give them an opportunity to step up and produce.

People will rise up to a challenge if they feel others are willing to do the same. Are you providing them with challenging problems? In order to inspire them, give projects or problems that have real significance and purpose.

What are you doing to raise the expectations and productivity of your team?

If they were never good, you can still raise your expectations, and when they don't meet your standard, it's time to let them go so they can find a better place for their skill set.

Chapter 2 Notes:

1. Ivey Business Journal (2006).
    http://www.iveybusinessjournal.com/topics/the-workplace/what-engages-employees-the-most-or-the-ten-cs-of-employee-engagement#.VDv3utJ0zIV
2. Aubrey Daniels International (2014).
    http://aubreydaniels.com/discretionary-effort
3. Annie Mueller (2015).
    http://www.engageforsuccess.org/about/what-is-employee-engagement.

Chapter 3
Develop Trust Relationships

Rule #1: Develop Trust Relationships

As with all relationships, employee engagement begins with trust. You may seek to implement various strategies and methods to increase productivity and your company's ROI, but without establishing a trust relationship with your employees, most of these techniques will fall short of your expectations or be temporary fixes.

He Said Yes!

Have you ever been in a conversation with someone and you couldn't quite understand what was going on?

My two older sons are now 10 and 8. A few years ago, my middle son, Sammy bounded into my office and started a conversation. Like any good father, I told him "not now, I'm busy." But he didn't give up. He patiently sat and waited for me to finish so we could chat. Once I realized he wasn't leaving, I decided to multi-task. I'm "listening" to him babble on about something while still doing work.

I have multiple screens up, I'm checking emails, the Master's leaderboard, and other highly important things. Just to show him I'm not a complete deadbeat, I gave him some rote responses like, "uh huh" "yeah sure, that sounds interesting" and "well, what does your mother say?"

Finally, he abruptly ends the conversation and says *thanks for talking Dad, you're so fun.*

At first I felt a little guilty, but then I thought to myself, you know what? I am fun. I am a fun dad.

Then he says, *Dad I love you, you're the best dad in the world.* He's so darn cute.

And he's right. I am the best dad in the world.

It was a Hallmark moment.

As I basked in the glow of my exceptional parenting skills, Sammy quickly ran upstairs and shouted to his older brother "He said YES!!!"

I was slapped back to reality.

Wait. What just happened?

What did I just say yes to??

I dropped everything and quickly ran upstairs after Sammy. The boys were so excited because they had just received my permission to do something they never thought would get approval. Which worried me.

Boys, what are you doing?

Sammy says, we're doing what you said we could do.

Okay, and what is that exactly?

And then I see it – taped across their room are multiple drawings of an American Ninja Warrior-style obstacle course where participants (my sons) are going to jump off the roof onto a trampoline and swim through shark-infested waters to a climbing rope that's been set on fire.

It was magnificent.

But completely hazardous and irresponsible. I couldn't let them follow through with their plans, even though I had said yes.

Employee engagement is a two-way street.

Were my sons engaged? Absolutely. Was I engaged? Not at all.

There is a cost to not being engaged. You lose the trust of your people. You miss out on important little details. Your ability to reason, negotiate, and compromise are drastically reduced.

Who's In Your Network?

Think of your closest and most significant relationships. They could be both personal and professional. You probably have a few people that immediately come to mind.

If you're like most people you've thought of your immediate family. Your parents, siblings, spouse, significant others, children or grandchildren, old high school and college friends, and your colleagues at work.

Why is this? You depend on them. You have deep bonds that go beyond the superficial. You know each other's faults and shortcomings, and yet the relationship thrives. There is a level of comfort and familiarity that comes with time, experience, and consistency. You trust them.

When I asked you to think of your closest and most important relationships, you probably didn't think of your grocer, your banker, or your primary care physician. Yet, if you were to look at the services these relationships provide: food, money, and healthcare, in reality you probably couldn't survive without these people. The strength of the relationship doesn't depend on what you can get out of the relationship. The strength of the relationship depends on a mutual bond of trust, developed over time and shared experiences.

Favorite Place in the World

Think of your favorite places in the world.

These responses may vary, but for most people they will say a vacation destination they love to visit or a restaurant that has significant meaning.

Wherever your favorite places are (bookstore, beach, coffeehouse, eatery), these are actual locations you've been to before, right? No one has ever said, my favorite place is <enter place you've never been before>. Ok, Captain Obvious, you just asked us to name our favorite place.

Think about it. Why is this your favorite place? You should have a multitude of reasons, but the primary one is you've been there before. You know it. It's not just an image in a brochure or magazine, it's a real place.

You've experienced it firsthand. All of your five senses have experienced this place and you can close your eyes and envision it right now. It's the difference between seeing something on TV and being there. It's like browsing the beach house on a website versus standing in front of the ocean and feeling the soft white sand between your toes. Most of us reserve our strongest recommendations for places we've actually been to. We trust our own experiences.

People will decide to follow you or not based on their level of trust they have in you.

Transfer of Trust

After your own personal experience, the next thing people trust are what other people say. Think about this. When you purchase something from eBay or Amazon, most people will first read what other people say about the product. Consumers are much more likely to make a buying decision based on how many 5 star ratings that product has than the actual information provided by the company. While you don't necessarily know any of these anonymous raters, we are much more likely buy a product because other people have effectively "vouched" for the merchandise. This buying decision is more significantly impacted when the rating or recommendation is from someone we know, like, and trust – but even with people we don't know, we're more likely to buy when a product has positive external ratings. This is called the transfer of trust.

We don't want to be sold to, but we do like to buy things we believe will help us.

In fact, there is research that shows we are willing to pay a premium for the exact same product if the ratings for that seller are higher than the lower cost seller. This is the power of trust. [1]

Companies know this and are desperately trying to replicate or manufacture "trust" with their consumers. This is almost impossible and comes off as a disingenuous attempt to buy someone's loyalty.

Developing trust with your team is the same challenge. There are no shortcuts. Trust can't be bought. There's no quick turnaround.

Developing trust takes time.

So how do you develop long-term and sustainable trust relationships?

Trust Tip #1: Be Good At Your Job

"70% of employees who lack confidence in their senior leadership are disengaged." [2]

Have you ever had a job where you felt like you could do a better job than your boss? Can you remember taking a class with a professor who knew less than you did about the subject? It's unsettling. You lack confidence in their leadership because they lack competence at their jobs.

As a leader, you can't rest on your laurels. Whether you are responsible for managing one employee or a team of 1,000 you have to good at your job. You have to be more than just competent, you should set the example by being someone they can learn from and emulate.

2 Simple Ways to Show You're Good at Your Job:

1. **Lead by example** – Don't ask your employees to do something you're not willing to do. If you need to stay extended hours then show them you will too. If you want them to learn new technology skills, show them you're willing to go to classes to learn as well.

2. **Coach them, don't lecture them** – Offer to help by showing them rather than just telling them what to do. Walk your employees through a job process. If they don't get it, ask them where in your example you need to be clearer so they do get it.

> **"People don't care how much you know until they know how much you care."**
>
> **~ Teddy Roosevelt**

Trust Tip # 2: Care

"Isn't it enough that they get a paycheck?"

That's the question I usually get when I speak with small business owners and managers about developing trust relationships with their team.

My answer is always, "yes" if you want employees to do the bare minimum. Remember, we're talking about engaging your employees so they use their discretionary effort to add value to your business.

In order for your employees to exert discretionary effort, they need to know you care for them.

Does this mean you are suddenly best friends and attend each other's kids' dance recitals? Don't be ridiculous. I don't even go to my own kid's events. It does mean you have to shift your view so you see your employees as more than just small cogs in a wheel or line item budget cuts.

It's not about fabricating intimacy, it's about seeing your co-workers as people. Real people with real lives away from work.

So how do you show them you care?

4 Ways to Show C.A.R.E for Your Team:

1. **Complete Person** – Care about their personal life as well as what they can do for you as an employee. Find out what makes them who they are. What are their hobbies, interests, and life goals? Be careful not to cross any boundaries, but seek to view them as a complete person rather than just another replaceable part in your system.

2. **Awareness** – Be aware of all the responsibilities an employee may have. If they didn't complete an assigned task, was it because they were lazy, did they forget, or did you ask them to do something else that took time away from their current objective? Be aware. Employees will most likely not be able to say no if you ask them to do something.

3. **Real** – Be real and relatable with your employees. No one is "above" anyone else. If someone is struggling at work or with their job and you can relate, then be open and honest and help them overcome their challenges. Again, show them don't just tell them what to do.

4. **Experiences** – Pay attention to what an employee is really good at. They may be looking for new experiences and if you pigeon-hole them to this one area, they will be looking to leave soon.

Reputation Economy

Employees learn fairly quickly whether their supervisor can follow through on a promise or not. People talk. Stories are shared. Especially within the age of social media, stories can live forever in short tweetable quips.

We live in a reputation economy. Once you break a promise or fail to follow through on a negative consequence, that trust seal is breached. Alas the old adage is true: what happens in Vegas, ends up on Facebook.

Imagine a supervisor that has designed a creative bonus incentive plan for workers to put forth extra effort, work evenings, and weekends in order to get the project done before month's end.

Everyone is excited and working together to meet the objectives and achieve their goals. After the month is over, the project comes to a successful close and the employees gather in the conference room to congratulate each other and to share in the good news.

Now imagine that same supervisor sheepishly walking into the room and explaining that due to budget cuts, there will be no bonuses after all. He thanks everyone for their hard work and doing all that was asked, but then admits there is no way he can award the promised bonuses.

Do you think there will be any takers for any future bonuses?

Don't make promises you can't keep.

Follow Through On Your Promises... and Your Consequences

Have you ever seen the bratty child at the grocery store demanding everything within their grubby fingers' reach? Then you've seen my kids. I'm sorry.

For the sake of argument, let's think of another child. Let's call him Little Johnny. Johnny has no care in the world but to conquer and destroy his parent's soul. And the lollipop at the checkout lane. That's it. Johnny wants two things: a human soul and that lollipop.

Johnny's mom is exhausted and weary. She summons up one last breath of courage and warns, "if you continue to cry and scream, we will be leaving this store right now! I mean it. I'm going to count to three and we're out of here. One... two... thrrrreeeeeeeeeee..."

You know exactly how this story plays out.

The parent caves. She appeases the soul-destroying lollipop-devouring child and apologetically pays for the groceries and swiftly leaves the store.

I openly admit I am this parent. Not all the time, but I've been known to give an infinite number of warnings only to give in at the eleventh hour. I just don't follow through with my consequences.

Why? Because it's so much easier just to give in. It's so much simpler to just give the little urchin his lollipop and small piece of your soul than to use every challenge as a teachable moment.

What this does is trade short-term relief for long-term grief.

Your employees have learned to act in accordance to your responses.

> **What gets recognized gets repeated.**

Chapter 3 Notes:

1. Ba, S. & Pavlou, P. A. (2002). Evidence of the effect of trust building technology in electronic markets: Price premiums and buyer behavior. *MIS Quarterly,* Vol. 26(3), pp. 243-268.
2. Dale Carnegie Training Institute.

Chapter 4

Establish a Feedback Loop

Rule #2: Establish a Feedback Loop

E mployees crave feedback. Not necessarily always a public declaration of how awesome they are – they just want some recognition that they're doing a good job.

> **"Catch someone doing something right."**
> **~ Ken Blanchard**

The Wedding Singer

A few years ago I was asked to be the singer for my friend's wedding ceremony. I was honored to be a part of this special day for this young couple. For this particular wedding, I was asked to sing "The Prayer" a song made popular by Celine Dion and Andrea Bocelli.

I had never heard the song before.

If you don't know the song, it's beautiful. But there's a slight problem, half the lyrics are in Italian. It's a duet and the half that's in Italian is the guy part. My part. I don't know Italian.

So I quickly emailed the bride, Lisa (*not her real name) to let her know my part of the song was in Italian. She said, "*I know, isn't that beautiful? It's my favorite part.*"

Okay then, glad we had that talk.

Time to start memorizing a bunch of foreign syllables and work on my best impersonation of Andrea Bocelli. No problem. I wore that CD out. I must have played that song every day for several hours, 30 days straight.

I wanted to get this song right. No shortcuts here. I couldn't fake my way through this song, even if others wouldn't know if I messed up – Lisa would know and so would I. My reputation was on the line. I easily spent over 60-70 hours listening, memorizing, enunciating, and practicing this song. I practiced in the car, shower, and wherever else I could belt this song without fear of ridicule.

Finally after a month, I had it down. I was nervous but I felt as ready as I could be.

The wedding was beautiful. The song turned out better than I expected. My duet partner was fantastic. Overall, it was an incredible experience. Many people came up afterwards to thank me for singing their favorite song and I received multiple inquiries for other weddings. I couldn't believe it, by some miracle, I had pulled it off.

Before we left town, my wife and I swung by the local grocery store near the church. I was still dressed in my suit and out of the corner of my eye, I noticed a man dressed in a tuxedo. He gave me a double take and immediately I knew who it was. It was the father of the bride! I was feeling pretty good about myself and thought I'd bask in the glow of some more praise in front of my admiring wife. I made my way across the busy grocery aisle to make sure we greeted each other.

As we shook hands – he gave me a quizzical stare and asked, "I know we've met before, now what is your name again?"

I paused.

Uh… my name is Phil.

"Ah, yes – that's right. Now where do I know you from?"

I'm friends with your daughter, Lisa.

"That's right! Well Phil, isn't that a coincidence you're in town, did you happen to know my daughter just got married today? Isn't that wonderful?"

I could feel my wife's hand squeeze my elbow as if to say, *don't say a word, Phil.*

I was stunned.

Didn't he didn't he know I was just in the wedding ceremony?! I could feel the tightening of my wife's vice grip, I quickly responded with a *"Congratulations Mr. So-n-So – please tell Lisa congratulations for me."*

"I will Phil, great to see you again!"

Now at this point, all I could think about was – are you kidding me? I just gave the performance of a lifetime in this man's daughter's wedding. Did he even hear me sing? I sang words in fluent Italian. I'm Korean! Isn't there some sort of uniqueness factor going on here?

Don't get me wrong, I wasn't expecting this man to bow before me and throw a parade in my honor, but the fact that he had no idea that I was the wedding singer, bugged me.

Funny thing. Before this interaction, I was on cloud nine. The wedding was beautiful, I sang a beautiful song, and everyone *else* recognized my artistic genius in its true glory.

Why should it even bother me that he didn't recognize me?

I craved recognition. And I didn't realize it *until I didn't get it.*

Your employees are the same way. They don't expect you to stop the presses when they do something right, but when was the last time you acknowledged their contributions? When was the last time you caught someone doing something right and thanked them for it?

Most people are going about their day doing their jobs because they know they're supposed to. There are even some employees that go beyond what's expected of them.

How often do you go out of your way to recognize their efforts and acknowledge them for their work? It doesn't have to be a public display either. A simple and quiet thank you or expression of your gratitude goes a long way towards engaging your employees.

If you don't provide your employees with feedback and recognition, they will eventually find an employer that does. You will think that they are leaving your organization to work for a company that's a "better cultural fit." But they are leaving because they feel underappreciated. They feel this way because no one consistently provides positive feedback and appreciation for their work.

Get into the habit of creating a positive feedback loop before your best people leave.

Notice I said nothing about new incentives, higher pay, or even a better parking spot. Employees feel more valued and satisfied when you recognize their work and let them know how much you appreciate them.

> "Appreciate everything your associates do for the business. Nothing else can quite substitute for a few well-chosen, well-timed, sincere words of praise. They're absolutely free and worth a fortune."
>
> ~ Sam Walton

Think of one employee this week that you can thank for providing excellent and consistent service and value to your organization. Now consider a small gesture of personal gratitude you can express in simple but meaningful way. Observe how this impacts their performance going forward. It will create a positive feedback loop.

Constructive Feedback

The next question I usually get is this: Does that mean you can't provide any formative or corrective feedback?

Of course you have to give both positive and constructive feedback. We all need practical and developmental feedback. There have to be moments where you can coach and mentor your employees to be better at their jobs.

Keep in mind that our brains are already wired towards a negativity bias.

I first wrote about the human propensity to have a negativity bias in my other book, *Chase One Rabbit*. But it bears repeating here. If I were to ask you to think of five areas of

. *r* life that you'd want to change or improve upon, you'd probably come up with ten. Now, if I asked you to think of the top five things you absolutely love about yourself, most individuals would be hard-pressed to find three. People are more likely to gravitate towards a negative view of themselves and are more easily able to recall negative instances than positive experiences. This also means, people have a tendency to remember more negative events in their lives than positive ones.

According to a report by the *Harvard Business Review*, when asked to recall emotional events, respondents reported four negative memories to every one positive memory. You are 80% more likely to recall a negative memory than a positive one. [2]

At the end of every course I teach, the students complete evaluation sheets. For the most part, I've been able to get fairly good evaluations from my students, but every once in a while I will get a not-so-flattering review. I know, crazy right?

It will say something to the effect of, "way too much busy work" or "this class was a complete waste of my time." Ouch. There could be 24 other positively glowing remarks about my course, but the one or two negative comments are the ones I remember. And it can really have an impact on my day.

Your Brain Makes You Stupid

The problem is we as humans have an immediate and emotional response to criticism. Some may be more prone to emotional responses than others, but biologically we can't help it. It's our brains way of telling us something is wrong and we have to protect ourselves. The emotional part of our brain, the limbic system lights up when we are in danger. Daniel

Goleman in his book *Emotional Intelligence* calls this the "Amygdala Hijack." [3]

The emotional response our brains have when we walk in the woods and encounter a hungry mountain lion is controlled by the amygdala (emotional brain), which rushes blood to our core and provides extra blood to our fast twitch muscle fibers so we can fight or flight. For survival purposes, this emotional process circumvents our neo-cortex (rational brain) which is responsible for logic and reasoning. When you're trying to survive a hungry mountain attack, you don't care whether your shoes match your socks. You just run. That's the amygdala's job to keep you alive.

Fortunately, most of us don't have to contend with mountain lions or natural predators in our daily work lives.

But we still have to contend with a daily commute, rush hour, a mortgage, and we deal with coworkers, conflicts, and deadlines. Some would say we're in much worse shape than our ancestors. I don't know about that, but I'm pretty sure one year's worth of traffic congestion and road rage is responsible for more stress and health issues than the history of all mountain lion-related fatalities combined.

Goleman explains even further, when we are in a fit of road rage, our ability to think rationally and logically is <u>severely compromised</u> and we become dumb, it's as if our IQ dropped 50 points. In other words, when your brain is emotionally charged as a result of a negative event (e.g., speeding ticket, unexpected bill, or bad employee review) – your ability to be rational plummets. Your emotional brain makes you stupid.

Power of the Pause

We have to actively train our brains not to overreact to negative stimuli. Our amygdalas can't help the initial response, that's biological, but you can be more intentionally aware of your negativity bias, and actively remind yourself to pause. The pause allows for your rational brain to kick in.

Pause for a minute before responding in an emotionally charged state. Pause and think before you hit the send button. Pause for a few minutes when you feel negative statements are truer than positive statements.

Recently I read a review of my book from a student and it said:

"Well-written, funny, and uplifting, but at times ran a little long."

Guess what my eyes gravitated towards?

Yep, that little jerk thought my book was a little long. *Well maybe if your pea-brain could handle big words you wouldn't find it such a daunting read.*

Not really. This was my initial response, but I was able to pause and thank them for their feedback. But remember, we are already inclined to give more power to negative feedback than we are to the positive feedback.

Keep this in mind as you provide constructive assessments for your employees.

A recent study in Psychology Today pointed to a 5 to 1 ratio of positive to negative statements. [4]

> **The human paradox is people remember criticism but respond to praise.**

Don't Ignore Them

You know what's worse than giving too much negative feedback? That's right – when you ignore your employees and give no feedback at all.

According to Gallup, the impact of negative feedback reduces employee engagement from 61% down to 45%.

Not surprising that negative feedback reduces engagement.

What's astounding is what happens when you ignore them. That same 61% level of engagement now *drops down to measly 2%* when there is no feedback at all.

Let that sink in.

The best way to cultivate trust and engagement is to provide positive to negative feedback with a ratio of 5:1 (5 Positive: 1 Constructive). The next best method is just to provide any feedback with no consideration of the negativity bias. At least you're showing that you have some interest in their development.

The worst thing you can do is ignore your people.

When you ignore someone, what you're communicating is "I don't care." You'd rather spend that time with other things or improving other people and therefore, you are telling your ignored employee "you no longer matter."

Employee engagement drops precipitously when you ignore someone. It will be difficult to maintain the trust and rapport you've built up to this point.

Don't ignore your people, they deserve better than that. And so do you.

Chapter 4 Notes:

1. Harvard Business Review
2. Psychology Today (2003). https://www.psychologytoday.com/articles/200306/our-brains-negative-bias.
3. Daniel Goleman. (1996). Emotional Intelligence: Why It Can Matter More Than IQ. Bantam Books.
4. Kumar, A. & Meenakshi, N. (2010). Organizational Behaviour: A Modern Approach. New Delhi: Vikas Publishing.

Chapter 5

Create a Culture of Accountability

Rule #3: Create a Culture of Accountability

Do you have a job description? Have you recently thought about your job description?

Most people chortle (yes, chortle) when I ask them to provide me with their job description, because they have no clue if they still have one. They know a generic job description exists *somewhere*, but it's been years since they've seen it. Most employees feel what they do often exceeds what the document states, so what's the point of worrying about a formal job description? It's useless.

So without a formal job description, how do your employees know what is expected of them? And how do you measure their progress?

Here's a method by Life Hacker CJ Goulding that I have found to be highly effective and easy to understand. It's called the S.I.M.P.L.E. method of employee accountability. [1]

The steps for creating a culture of accountability are S.I.M.P.L.E:

1. Set expectations

2. Invite commitment
3. Measure progress
4. Provide feedback
5. Link to consequences
6. Evaluate effectiveness

#1: Set Expectations

As a leader, what are the clearly stated objectives for your people? If this isn't clear to you it won't be for them. The job description is a good place to start, but that doesn't provide any insights on the next step in the career path. If you're having trouble coming up with your own expectations, why don't you ask your employees to draft what their job duties and responsibilities are? Also ask how they see their career advancing. You might be pleasantly surprised by all they are doing. Or you may have new ideas for how they can expand their roles.

Creating a culture of accountability begins by setting clear expectations that provide a clear path for personal growth and career advancement.

#2: Invite Commitment

Once you've agreed upon the goals and expectations, it's a matter of mutually agreeing to abide by those objectives. In my classrooms and in my training workshops, I explain the syllabus is a contract between two parties: the instructor and the student. They are responsible for reading the syllabus and to complete the readings and assignments listed in the document. In return, I am responsible for grading, assessing, and teaching the material according to the syllabus. It's a collaborative commitment to act in concert with the stated goals. Of course things change and we have to adapt, but the written document invites joint commitment.

#3: Measure Progress

How do you measure progress? Are you going to be measuring on a daily, weekly, monthly, or quarterly progress report? You shouldn't go longer than monthly or quarterly without some reporting if you can help it. Obviously it becomes time-consuming if you have more than 50 people you are responsible for managing, and you will have consolidate and delegate some leadership responsibilities. Still, you will need to have an objective measure of what success looks like.

Set the quantitative metrics for progress and be consistent in reviewing the numbers. Keeping a quantitative metric (e.g., 30 new sales calls, 20% increase in revenue, or 10% reduction in returns) for measuring progress reduces confusion, bias, and subjectivity. Stick to the facts.

#4: Provide Feedback

Let them know how they're doing. Ask them how they think they're progressing. Their responses may surprise you. In many ways, they will be harder on themselves than you would be, so you will have to play the role of mentor or career coach. This is a lot more fun and effective than being the enforcer. And remember the natural tendency to the negativity bias.

#5: Link to Outcomes

Have a clear linkage between individual performance and rewards or consequences. Employees need to know what their progress (or lack thereof) means to their professional careers and the company's goals. Without this link, it becomes too easy for the employee to disengage. It's like a weight loss or investment savings program, you need to link daily and micro performance goals to overall outcome and end results.

#6: Evaluate Effectiveness

Evaluate how effective the goals are. Review the challenges or hurdles that have stopped progress and whether the plans have increased the level of accountability. Another key point is to not be afraid to adjust the plan as you go. Remember, progress is the name of the game. You won't reach all of your annual goals overnight, so temper your expectations and don't be afraid to adjust the metrics as you go.

Let Them See the Big Picture

My son Sammy and I love jigsaw puzzles. We can spend days or weeks working on a puzzle. With each puzzle, we've increased the difficulty level, but the payoff has been that much greater when we're finished.

You know what the most frustrating thing is about putting a puzzle together?

That's right a missing piece. Even with a 1000 piece puzzle, you could have 999 pieces in place, but that one last piece makes everything else seem worthless. Interesting, this only represents .001 of the entire image, but it can leave you feeling utterly unsatisfied.

Let your employees see the big picture.

Allow your employees to see the end product or service. We've all become such specialists within our own tiny fiefdoms that we fail to see how our little part impacts the bigger whole.

Let your employee see where the organization is going. Let them know what the short and long-term goals are.

> **Link individual goals to organizational success.**

If your employees aren't linking their individual puzzle piece into the greater mosaic, it's like trying to complete a huge puzzle without seeing the top of the box.

They become disengaged when they don't see the connection between what they do and where you're going.

Let them see, taste, and feel what your company's vision and mission are. Let them chew on it for a while. Help those individual employees see how their "small" part plays a role in the overall mission.

The Power of Purpose

Do you ever remember a time in your life or career when you realized it was all pointless? Perhaps you're there now.

You wake up, rush through the morning motions, multitask on your way to work, handle multiple projects that all require your immediate attention, have another "working lunch," scramble to reply to emails from last night, come home, dinner, TV, and go to sleep. Same thing next morning, rinse, and repeat.

What if we faced death every day?

I met a young man named Steve Sawyer when he came to my college campus (Indiana University of Pennsylvania) in 1998. It was incredible to hear him speak. He was only a year or two older than me, but he spoke with such power, wisdom, and purpose, it seemed as if he had lived a thousand years.

Steve knew he was going to die soon. He was born with hemophilia. Hemophilia is treated with blood transfusions. Between 1980 and 1983, he contracted the HIV virus and Hepatitis C through a series of over 100 blood transfusions. In 1990, when he was only 15, he was told that he had the HIV virus. During his senior year in high school he had his first serious bout with the virus. He lost 27 pounds in two weeks and his T-cell count was at 213 and falling. When T-cells drop below 200, you are considered to have full-blown AIDS. [2]

He prayed that God would heal him and miraculously he regained all his weight back and his T-cell counts jumped up to 365. In 1993, he began attending Curry College in Boston. But by 1995 he was too weak to continue with school. He had cirrhosis of the liver due to the virus.

Imagine the pain, anger, and despair most people would feel at this point. A young college kid trying to live his life with a fatal virus contracted through someone else's mistakes. How would you respond?

I would have been furious. Personally, I would have shaken my fist at God, the doctors, the nurses, and everyone else I could spew my wrath on. Steve chose a different path. That winter of 1995, Steve's life changed and he found a new sense of hope that he could share with others. He shared that he had become a Christian.

"I no longer had to go to bed every single night worrying about whether I was going to be alive the next day. I no longer had a fear of dying, because dying wouldn't just end in blackness.

Now when I die I know I would spend an eternity, forever, with the greatest love in the universe. It is so freeing."

What an incredible testimony. He found his purpose. Starting in 1995 to 1999, Sawyer traveled across the country telling his story and offering encouragement and hope to live life to the fullest.

A few months after we met in the fall of 1998, Steve became too weak to continue his campus speaking tours. In March 1999, Steve died of liver failure due to hepatitis C. In his final days, Steve's last wish was that he would be able to speak to one more campus.

Why? Hadn't he done enough?

He felt that if he could go to just one more campus, he could share his message of hope with one more person. He even said that if he had to get this disease in order for more people to hear his message of hope "then it is worth it. In light of eternity, that is all that matters."

Incredible. Even in the face of imminent death, he wanted to continue his journey. This is the power of purpose. And it changed hundreds if not thousands of lives across the country and even the world.

At the age of 23, Steve Sawyer died knowing that he lived the last four years of his life full of purpose. It fueled him. It energized him. To meet him, you would never guess a lethal virus was wrecking his internal organs. He was a dynamic speaker, energetic, and full of life.

Someone who faces death everyday has an appropriate perspective on how to live life this day. No one is guaranteed tomorrow. The unimportant things are put in their proper place, and the things that matter become the priority.

Without purpose our tendency is to overemphasize the inconsequential.

We spend a majority of our adult life in our companies, small businesses, and places of work. It is important for employees to feel a sense of purpose to what they are doing.

What Matters to You?

Think of a list of the top five things that matter to you.

My guess is your list won't be too different than mine. Perhaps, it's about having meaningful relationships with significant others and loved ones, or doing purposeful work that has a lasting impact, and having the means and the ability to enjoy time and experiences with friends and family. These things all have unique meaning to you because of who you are, but when it comes down to what's really important, we often long for similar things.

For most people, it's not about money and success, it's about relationships.

For most employees, it's not about wealth, prestige, or material things, it's about doing work that matters.

It's about creating experiences where employees can build relationships with each other and to contribute to a cause greater than their own. Apart from our families, most employees will be spending the majority of their prime working years in a place of employment. Engaged employees want to do work that matters.

What are you doing to create these types of experiences for your employees?

Service Learning

Every year, I implement a Service-Learning component into each of my classes. With no exceptions, my students will not remember the difference between a primary key and a foreign key within a relational database, but they will remember helping a local non-profit organization.

My students form mini-consulting groups to assist service-based organizations in their technology or social media marketing strategies. They get to put into practice what they learn in the classroom.

But more importantly they get to see the impact of what they do. People want to do work that matters. They want to believe their work is contributing to something bigger than themselves.

When you are able to link individual goals to organizational success and tie that to a greater sense of purpose, you've created an engaged workforce.

Chapter 5 Notes:

1. CJ Goulding. (2015).
    http://www.lifehack.org/articles/productivity/6-practical-
    ways-create-culture-accountability.html.
2. Steve Sawyer. (1998).
    http://www.everystudent.com/features/sawyer.html.

Chapter 6

Encourage Self-Direction

Rule #4: Encourage Self-Direction

Does anybody love being micro-managed?

Believe it or not, when I ask this question to my audiences, there will be a tiny smattering of people that raise their hands. I've heard some people explain to me that they need be micro-managed in order to be productive. I would argue they need clearer goals, reasonable timelines, and some mutual accountability.

For the majority of us, we hate being micro-managed. Like an untamed mule, we buck against any type of overly nitpicky boss that wants to dot every "I" and cross every "T." If you're constantly being directed and corrected by your supervisor, at a certain point, you are going to come to the conclusion that:

1. Management doesn't trust my ability, or
2. Management doesn't trust my integrity.

Neither thought feels good.

When was the last time someone gave you an important task or responsibility? Not just a menial chore but something of real value to your organization?

I Can Do It Myself

All three of my sons love tinkering around with tools. Ever since he was 2 years old, Sammy's been actively involved in everything I do. If I'm shoveling, he needs to shovel, if I'm mowing the lawn – guess who takes out his little Fisher-Price® mower?

As he's gotten a little older he wants do things on his own, without my help. Just a few years ago, he would wait until I gave him a task, but now he is the one who initiates the work. His latest kick is baking. He wants to break the eggs, he wants to beat the cake mix, he wants to grease the pan, set the oven, turn on the stove, and play with the knives, etc. At times I worry because I really like cake. I don't want egg shells in my cake.

He says, "Dad, don't worry, I can do it myself."

> **People need to know that their efforts are making an impact to the organization.**

Are you providing opportunities for your people to move up in responsibility and influence?

Intrinsic Motivation

In his book *Drive,* Daniel Pink describes autonomy as one of the key motivating factors for employees. Beyond money, vacation days, or a new gold watch (external motivation), people want to do work that is personally important to them. It's driven by an inner desire and strong sense of self. This is the power of intrinsic motivation. Of course, as a leader you will still need to assign specific tasks that relate to your organizational goals. However, even within this scenario – you can still encourage self-direction.

Here's how:

Give parameters, then offer choices.

Determine what the parameters of the project are and then offer a variety of choices for your employees to complete it. What is a project that you've been holding on to and waiting to delegate but just haven't pulled the trigger yet?

It should be something that is important for your company. Something that you've wanted to get done, but haven't had the time to do. It doesn't have to be your core mission-critical project, but it should be meaningful to the success of your organization.

Let's take for example a new social media marketing campaign that promotes a new product or service offering. You want your social media campaign to use various online channels that gives your company visibility at the local and national level.

There are a wide variety of applications and software platforms to use, but you might give the following parameters or guidance:

1. The organization's brand and message should be consistent across the top social media platforms of the time.
2. Create a sense of openness and dialogue with our community, but don't get too personal.

3. The social media campaign to be fun and creative, but also reasonably protect us against liability.

Give your employees clear parameters on what your project is and isn't. Then offer choices on how they choose to keep you updated on the progress of their work.

Make sure you are clear on what the level of feedback and accountability is going to be. In fact, let them tell you what this is going to look like. If this schedule of feedback and status updates fits both your needs and timelines, great! If not, feel free to tweak and come to a mutual understanding of what success looks like.

This provides enough autonomy to go out and do something meaningful, while still maintaining a level of quality and strategic control of the project.

The Mission Trumps the Method

We love our mobile apps don't we? As an MIS professor this can be an occupational hazard, but most of us can get enamored with the latest gadgets, mobile apps, and methodologies. We need a meeting planning app to check-in to our meetings to pre-plan our future meetings. In the age of smart devices and mobile apps, we start with the cool new way or methodology first to increase our productivity and this drives the new strategy. This is the tail wagging the dog.

We need to be clear on the mission first.

Engaged employees *need to be shown why* they're su,_
do something and then they can figure multiple ways to ge.
done.

Too Many Toys?

> How many people ruin themselves by laying out money
> on trinkets of frivolous utility? What pleases these
> lovers of toys is not so much the utility, as the aptness
> of the machines which are fitted to promote it. All their
> pockets are stuffed with little conveniences. They
> contrive new pockets, unknown in the clothes of other
> people, in order to carry a greater number. They walk
> about loaded with a multitude of baubles, in weight and
> sometimes in value inferior to an ordinary [box], some
> of which may sometimes be of some little use, and of
> which the whole utility is certainly not worth the
> fatigue of bearing the burden. [1]

This was written ***over 250 years ago*** by Adam Smith.

It still remains true today.

We become too easily enamored with the latest knick-knacks,
gadgets, and management fads. Are we introverts or
extroverts? Should we go to the cloud or keep our servers in-
house? I have Dropbox, but will it integrate with my Evernote
scheduler? Did you get my Snapchat?

Valid questions for sure, but if the method is driving the
mission, we have it backwards. Start with the mission, then
choose the method.

The mission trumps the method.

ROWE

Have you heard of the Results Only Work Environment (ROWE)?

Start re-thinking the 9-5 schedule.

ROWE is a management strategy that rewards employees based on their results (business objectives) rather than how many hours they've worked. Significant portions of the ROWE strategy have been implement at Best Buy, the Gap, and Mabel's Labels.

Employees are compensated based on their performance not their attendance. While some have criticized the strategy as just another way to increase telecommuting, others have found this method allows significant freedom and flexibility for the organization to focus on the bigger picture as opposed to just the daily routine.

ROWE may not work for everyone, however it's worth considering for those organizations or departments that are more nimble and have clear objectives, hard project deadlines, and transparent metrics that are easily measured.

Provide training relevant to their career goals.

One of the departments I used to work for was very proactive in their training. Whether it was in-house training, on-site training, or national conferences – my group was one of the most trained departments in the entire organization.

In fact, it wasn't until I left the organization for an opportunity to advance, that I realized how fortunate I was. It was a shock

for me when I left that company to work for *
the training budget was next to nothing.

All things being equal, given the choice betwee
organization that provides relevant and extensive training
programs versus little to no training programs, engaged
employees will always gravitate towards the training. Your
best people want to grow, learn, and be challenged at their jobs.

This proverbial anecdote is true:

**CFO asks his CEO, 'What happens if we invest in
developing our people and then they leave the company'**

CEO answers, 'What happens if we don't, and they stay?'

Have you worked with people who have quit their jobs while
still coming to work? Oh, they are still there collecting a
paycheck and draining the system, but they have effectively
checked out of their jobs. They have quit while working.

Provide timely and relevant training to your employees and
you will have a motivated and engaged workforce that will
want to stay.

Choose not to provide relevant training and you will wish they
had left.

ιapter 6 Notes:

1.   Adam Smith. (1759). The Theory of Moral Sentiments. (p.178).

Chapter 7

Inspire Innovation

Rule #5: Inspire Innovation

Our economy has evolved. Beyond the agricultural and industrial age and even beyond the information age, some economists are calling the next wave the conceptual or idea age. Ideas are the economic good for the future.

Think about that statement. Where is the best place for new and original ideas for your organization? I cringe when I envision executives hiring all manner of external consultants to craft new and exciting ideas before they think to tap into their own idea hubs. You need to encourage ideas and innovation from within your own workforce!

Ideas are the new commodity.

So how do we get these ideas?

Promote Collaboration

With our highly inter-connected environment, time and geography are no longer barriers to working together. We have unprecedented access to share ideas, projects, and challenges with our employees, peer groups, business partners, vendors, and clients. Yet, we are more siloed and isolated than ever before.

Are you actively seeking ways to collaborate with your valued partners?

> **Purposeful collaboration provides a rich platform for new insights and creativity to develop.**

Collaboration doesn't simply mean putting teams together. Purposeful collaboration is more intentional, has more buy-in, and creates a reciprocal sense of drive and direction. Purposeful collaboration should also increase diversity. By diversity, I don't necessarily mean racial or ethnic diversity (although it most likely could).

Your team should be encouraged to work with other people outside of their departments.

People who work with other people outside of their area of expertise tend to ask more "why" questions.

Diverse groups are more creative.

It reduces the likelihood of "group think" or "industry expert think." People who don't know a certain business practice will ask why it's done a certain way. These questions will force your employees to re-think the true purpose and meaning of why they do what they do.

Unusual Pairings Game

I play a short game called "Unusual Pairings" in each of my employee engagement workshops. I'll ask you to play right now.

Think of one appliance, tool, or gadget in your kitchen. Whatever pops into your mind first is it.

Now think of a tool or device you use to clean your house.

Got it?

Okay, now mash those two objects together to create a completely new tool or appliance.

1. What does it do?
2. How does it work?
3. What do you call it?
4. How much would it sell for?
5. How will you market it?

I will change the parameters of the game once in a while. Sometimes I will ask participants to think of a gadget in the bathroom, in their garage, or tools for lawn care. But the objective remains the same: combine two completely unrelated objects together to create a brand new one.

Throughout the years there have been some very creative tools and gadgets that have been borne out of these sessions. Some of my favorites are:

1. Chopsticks with an attached mini-fan to cool off noodles.
2. Refrigerator with embedded vacuum hose.

3. Butter dispensed through a roller stick (think glue stick that dispenses butter). I know right?

Creativity is unleashed whenever we make new connections.

Diverse City

Many cities are revitalizing their urban centers. There is an ongoing push for urban renewal within the U.S. and Canada where organizations, small businesses, and entrepreneurs are encouraged to relocate their operation centers back to the inner city.

The most successful urban revivals are those cities that are able to attract the most diverse groups of people. Areas with the most cultural and ethnic divergence also tend to have the most creative and innovate jobs and industry growth. It's somewhat of a self-fulfilling prophecy: when you have a diverse culture, there is a rise in diversity in the local businesses, restaurants, arts, and music, which attracts yet even more diverse groups – and the growth cycle continues. [1]

The same is true of your organization. The more diverse you are, the more creative you will be. This will lead to new and different perspectives on the way you operate as a business, which will attract even more diverse talent. It's a virtuous cycle.

Zappos is a classic example of this. Their core value remains the same: Be Obsessed with the Customer Experience. Their hiring and recruiting practices are completely different than the norm for other similar online retail businesses. They don't hire the same Harvard and MIT graduates with the 5-star resumes. They get resumes from all over the world. They could easily hire the same type of person over and over again, but this doesn't contribute to their mission of being obsessed with the customer experience. They want new and fresh viewpoints and outlooks from all types of people from various backgrounds. They are hiring Zebras and Ostriches.

Did you know that Zappos doesn't have a formal business dress code? You can come to work in pajamas and mohawk if that's what makes you most comfortable and productive. You also don't conform to a certain 9-5 norm. Some work well beyond the 40 hours required to get projects done, in fact most will – but it's not required. There is an abundance of discretionary effort.

They hire people to bring their unique skills, outlook, and background and they say, come as you are.

I realize this exact model may not work for many of the organizations I consult with, but the fact remains – diversity and collaboration are foundational steps to increase creativity and innovation within your organizations.

Encourage Curiosity

Have you ever noticed how many questions kids ask?

They ask tons of questions. All the time. Doesn't matter where you are: doctor's office, oil change, grocery line, etc. I could be on the phone with the President of Mars, my sons would be like, "Dad, can I just ask one quick question?"

But I am on the phone with Mars.

"But I really need your help with this Lego piece."

They don't give up. Especially my kids. From the moment they wake up all the way to bed, it's constantly, "just one more question…"

Kids are inherently curious. They want to learn. Everything is still a new and yet-to-be discovered adventure waiting to be unearthed.

What a fun way to live life!

I spent a few hours with Dr. David Cooperrider as he presented his findings from his book *Appreciative Inquiry* [2], and I was immediately reminded of the power of curiosity and recapturing our sense of wonder and inquisitiveness.

As we become adults and enter the "real world" – we've been trained to <u>find the one right solution to the problem</u> (*as if that really exists*). Once we have it, we move on. We stop looking. We stop asking.

> **"We keep moving forward, opening new doors, and doing new things, because we're curious and curiosity keeps leading us down new paths."**
>
> **~ Walt Disney**

A curious nature is critical in achieving creative and innovative breakthroughs in your work.

Don't settle for the status quo. Go for digging deeper.

Failure

How do you view failure? As a leader if you are someone who is constantly trying to eliminate mistakes and decrease inefficiencies, then you probably aren't going to encourage much innovation. This will work if your goal is compliance – but if you want to tap into the creative energy of your team, this is not the model to emulate.

You want a highly-engaged and enthusiastic workforce that is willing to stretch themselves and take on various roles to get the job done, right?

Then you have to put failure in its proper place.

> **"Failure is a learning experience, a rung on a ladder, a plateau at which to get your thoughts in order and prepare to try again."**
>
> **~ W. Clement Stone**

Play the What If Game

Here's a fun way to exercise your curiosity: play the "What If" game.

It's simple, ask the question "What if..." and apply it a specific issue or situation at work that you want to improve or change.

In my first year of teaching, I was tasked with teaching a course entitled, Operations Management. For most students this was a very challenging and boring class as it reinforced concepts they learned in Quantitative Methods and

Analysis. Even if you're a numbers geek, this was not going to be a fun course.

Here's the "What If?" I did for my class: "What if there was a fun way to teach my Operations Management class so that students will learn and apply the concepts and won't want to kill me?"

With that question in my mind, I got some responses back from my colleagues, former and current students, and hatched the plan.

I designed the course around the creating, planning, and building of a physical board game. They had to brainstorm and work in teams to build a board game from scratch. They had to create the rules, write a rule book, design a mock-up, and then source the materials, create a prototype, and finally determine the best pricing and marketing strategies. There were 4 teams and the goal was for each team to compete for the most pre-sales by the end of the semester.

They were creating a brand new game to sell to the market. In the meantime, they were learning and applying theories and concepts related to operations management, supply chains, procurement, quality control, marketing, and logistics, but in a completely different, unique, and fun way.

One of my favorite creations was a gamed called "AniMath." This game uses the various categories and schema of the animal kingdom to teach grade school children the basic concepts of multiplication. This group even created slick marketing material to promote their game.

It was a blast. The What-If Game and competition provided memorable learning experiences for both me and my students.

What is one way for you to reawaken your curiosity?

Encourage your team to be curious. It's a long lost art and we need to encourage and promote curiosity in our organizations. One of the best ways to grow in curiosity is to challenge the status quo. Not simply for the sake of being contrarian, but to truly look at a problem and ask:

1. Why are we doing this?
2. How does that work?
3. What happens when we don't do this?
4. What if we could this instead?
5. What do our best (or worst) customers think?

Have "Why" Teams

There are multiple Fortune 500 companies that have started "Why Groups" or "Why Engineers." These groups are responsible for hammering away at new ideas, services, and problems the organization is working through. They have no vested interest other than to ask why and hopefully make the product or service better.

What are the ideas or business problems that you'd like a new and fresh perspective on?

Provide a brief description of the problem to your "Why Team" and let them ask away. Don't be surprised if they ask very basic "why" questions in the beginning. Be patient. As they dig deeper – there's going to be a temptation to simply say, "because that's just the way it is!"

Well, why is it "just the way it is?" How did that idea originate? What if we tried something else?

Don't stop asking questions until you reach a new insight or new perspective you had not considered before.

Keep Going

Keep going, even when you don't see immediate results.

As a writer, this has been one of the most valuable lessons for me. In writing you can't wait to write only when the muse appears or else you'll be at the whimsy of whenever she decides to grace you with her presence..

What has worked for me is to commit to writing a little bit every day. Even if it's just 15 minutes a day. This forces my subconscious brain to think about my writing and gives my mind and thoughts a chance to make new connections throughout every day, rather than only on the days I feel "inspired."

I even started a blog called: write15minutes.com.

I've heard it said that inspiration is overrated.

I tend to agree, but I would modify it to "**waiting for inspiration is overrated.**"

> **Innovation is more about deliberate practice and effort than it is about waiting for that Eureka moment.**

We are far more likely to be inspired if we're committed to working on a consistent basis.

Chapter 7 Notes:

1. Richard Florida. (2011).
   http://www.citylab.com/work/2011/12/diversity-leads-to-economic-growth/687.
2. David Cooperrider & Diana Whitney. (2006). Appreciative Inquiry: A Positive Revolution in change. Berrett-Koehler Publishers.

Conclusion

Be Vigilant

Employee Engagement is a process. Think of it as a continuum rather than a single destination or point in time.

The Ice Cream Will Melt

Growing up in Philadelphia, my parents had a 7-11 convenience store located on 46th and Walnut Street. The heart of West Philadelphia. Not the safest of neighborhoods, but this is where my parents could afford the rent payments, so there we were. I spent a lot of time at the 7-11 store because we didn't have things like "day care" or "kids play areas" growing up. You just did what your parents did. And if you complained, you sat in the car.

After enough times of being sent to the car, I decided I was going to help. My job was to keep the store clean. Any trash, change, cigarette butts were my responsibility and I got to keep the loose coins I picked up. The best part? I got to eat as much ice cream as I wanted.

The only rule was the ice cream had to be one day past the expiration date and no one else was going to buy it. I kept my eye on those expiration dates like a hawk (or ostrich). If you know anything about me, it's that I love ice cream. I mean seriously, I love it.

One summer day in the early 1980s, there was a huge storm and the power on the whole block of Walnut Street went out. Our diesel generator would kick in soon, but this would only last a few hours.

The margins within the convenience store world are pretty thin. One of the places this is especially true is with the frozen foods. Once you factor in spoilage, breakage, theft, and the cost of inventory space – it becomes a nickel and dime enterprise.

Did I mention my fondness for ice cream?

So the one and only thing my mother says before she goes to lock the door is, "Philip, whatever you do, don't open the freezer doors, or else the ice cream will melt!"

Right. Got it mom. No problem, I can handle this.

Hold up.

What?

The ice cream is going to melt?! The horror. My six-year-old mind could hardly fathom all that ice cream going to waste. My precious ice cream was going to melt outside of my stomach.

I was determined to prevent this catastrophe.

I jumped and grabbed a spoon and pulled out several pints of my favorite ice cream. I figured it was all going bad, so I might as well start with the good stuff. I also went all in with the most expensive brands that my mom would never let me eat. I had to be quick. I had already wolfed down multiple helpings of Haagen-Dazs® Rum Raisin and Butter Pecan and Ben and Jerry's Cherry Garcia before I could hear my mother yelling at me over my ice cream haze.

"Stop!" my mom screamed, "what do you think you're doing?!"

I explained that I was doing my duty by consuming the perishable goods before they spoiled.

Exasperated, my mother lifted her hands in frustration and starting cursing in Korean.

The good news was the power outage only lasted 20 minutes.

The bad news was I successfully "saved" about 6 pints of the really expensive stuff.

I went from being dutiful son and free labor to profit margin destroyer.

Be Vigilant

You may think after a while that you have employee engagement all figured out, but remember it's a process not a destination. If you have already implemented some employee engagement strategies, you are probably better off than over half your competition, but don't rest there.

You may believe you have everything under control, but when an unexpected disaster, obstacle, or power outage hits your organization are you ready for your employees to be as committed to your organization as you are?

There is no magic bullet. The best companies realize this and are consistently engaging their employees through various approaches. More recently, there has been a push for corporate citizenship, corporate culture, and mission or values-based initiatives, but the language is all very similar. These organizations are all seeking to establish and increase their levels of employee engagement.

As a recap, here are the 5 Rules of Employee Engagement:

> Rule #1: Develop Trust Relationships
> Rule #2: Establish a Feedback Loop
> Rule #3: Create a Culture of Accountability
> Rule #4: Encourage Self-Direction
> Rule #5: Inspire Innovation

Every 18 Months

In 2000 I graduated with a Bachelor's degree from Indiana University of Pennsylvania (IUP) and a Certificate in Computer Programming from Computer Learning Centers, which is a technology school in Pittsburgh, PA. The turnover trend for all Information Technology-related jobs was about 18 months. Due to the growing nature of the industry, contract positions, and the increasing need for new talent, the 18 month turnover rate has not changed much in the past 15 years. As I look back on my previous jobs, the longest I have stayed with one company was a little over 4 years.

In the coming 2015-16 Academic Year, I will be starting my sixth year here at Walsh University. I'm convinced that I've spent more hours in the office and served on more committees here at Walsh than in any of my other employers combined, but I've never felt more engaged.

Here are how the 5 Rules of Employee Engagement work for me here:

Rule #1 – Trust: I trust my supervisor, the senior leadership of the university, and the colleagues I work with.

Rule #2 – Feedback Loop: From day one, I've had a clear path for growth and I know what is expected of me.

Rule #3: – Culture of Accountability: I can see how my small role fits within the overall mission of the organization. I have a strong sense of purpose to what I do.

Rule #4: – Self-Direction: I have a high level of autonomy and have choices within reasonable parameters.

Rule #5: – Innovation: I am encouraged to innovate, research, and try new things inside and out of the classroom. Failure is just part of the process of growing and developing my career.

I enjoy the challenge of research, classroom instruction, student advising, and working with my co-workers and the administration.

This is where I belong. It is hard work, but I love what I'm doing. I have a strong sense of purpose that I'm serving the greater good and I have an opportunity to contribute to the mission of the university.

May Not Fit Everyone

You may implement these rules and still find people are not engaged or committed to growing with your organization. That's okay. As long as you are clear about your expectations and standards for success, this process will be a way for people to "self-select" out.

I have peers and colleagues that teach information technology and other highly transferable skills within higher education that still adhere to the "move every couple of years" rule in order to advance their careers and make more money.

You can't win everybody over.

Some People Just Want to Make Beer

I have a good friend, Jay, who is an excellent teacher. He's taught in the public school system in Pittsburgh for the past five years. Before that he was teaching in Maryland for a few years. He's earned a Master's Degree in Education, all the appropriate certifications and licensures to teach, and he's a tenured faculty member. He's really good at his job. He has a bunch of reasons to just coast for the rest of his career.

But his dream is to make beer. Great dream right?

In 2015 he and his business partners have officially started a local brewing company in their hometown. It's called Levity Brewing Company (levitybrewing.com) and their tagline is: *Serious Beer for the Light at Heart.* I love that. It fits their personalities so well.

My guess is even if Jay were completely engaged at work as a public school teacher, he would have still followed his dream and started a brewery. Sometimes you do everything you can and your best people still leave.

Give them your blessing and let them go. You don't want burnt bridges to prevent them from coming back if things change, or to tarnish your name and influence for recruiting new talent in the future. Remember we live in the reputation economy.

Small wins

Employee engagement should be considered at all levels within your organization.

My goal is to help leaders understand, recognize, and consider how they can implement these five rules to increase employee engagement within their companies.

Begin with any one of the five rules you naturally gravitate towards. Note, while they are all important, if you don't establish a trust relationship with your employees, all of the other rules won't be as effective.

There are those in your organization that just "get it." Through no intentional persuasion, these are your early devotees. Can you leverage their enthusiasm and energy to rally the other troops?

Don't be overwhelmed or discouraged by all you have yet to do. Even the best companies are constantly retooling and re-establishing how to increase their employee engagement.

Celebrate the small wins and build on what you're already doing well.

Your Zebras and Ostriches

Your employees are your first customers. Your employees are your most important customers. If your team doesn't believe in your mission, your customers won't.

Make sure you are developing key leaders in each of your strategic positions. Take the time to get to know them. Actively seek out opportunities to mentor, guide, and develop them. Encourage the innovators and collaborators to try new things.

It's time for you to start hiring the best Zebras and Ostriches for your organization and let them feed off of each other's strengths.

If you have any questions, comments, or thoughts – I'd love to hear from you! Please feel free to email me at pkim@walsh.edu.

I look forward to hearing about your employee engagement journey!

Philip Kim Biography:

 Dr. Philip Kim is an educator, speaker and consultant. Phil has been published in over 20 academic journals and has been invited to present his research at both national and international conferences. As a speaker and consultant he has worked with over 50 small to mid-sized institutions including higher education, financial services, and non-profit organizations.

Before becoming a business professor at Walsh University, Phil served as the Vice President of Information Security for a $5B financial services organization, where he was responsible for managing the bank's information security environment and engineered the bank's internal IT risk management practices. □

Raised by first generation Korean immigrants, Phil has worked at all of his parents businesses including 7-11 convenience stores, gas stations, diners, and restaurants. He understands the value of hard work and education. His passion is to use his knowledge and expertise to help others achieve their life's goals one small win at a time.

You can visit Phil at his blog at:
www.write15minutes.com.

Chase One Rabbit:

"You won't be able to put this book down! No matter what change you want to make in your life, these words will empower you to begin today and stick with it. Not only are the principles incredibly powerful...Phil uses illustrations that engage your heart as well as your mind! Life-changing!"

■ **Glenna Salsbury, CSP, CPAE, Author of *The Art of The Fresh Start***

*Available for purchase on Amazon here:

http://www.amazon.com/Chase-One-Rabbit-Failure-Success/dp/1500823007/ref=tmm_pap_title_0

Book Phil to speak at your next event:

<u>Seminars, Workshops, and Speeches:</u>

- **Chase One Rabbit: The Top 3 Strategies to Develop Your Own Success Habits**
  - Productivity and Professional Development
- **5 Rules for Employee Engagement and Developing Your Own People**
  - Employee Engagement
- **What's Your EQ? The 5 Factors of Emotional Intelligence and How it Impacts Your Leadership**
  - Emotional Intelligence and Leadership
- **Get Clients Now! ™ - Licensed Sales Training Program – (Available as a training workshop and a 28 day coaching program)**
  - Sales Training Workshop and Coaching Program

Contact Phil to book your next event.

330-244-4690 * <u>pkim@walsh.edu</u>

Made in the USA
Middletown, DE
18 May 2015